The Catalyst Code

Psychology, Volume 4

Dr.Raam Harvard

Published by Poverty Eradication Trust (Triple ISO), 2025.

THE CATALYST CODE

First edition. September 24, 2025.

ISBN: 978-9349611610

Written by Dr.Raam Harvard.

Also by Dr.Raam Harvard

Money
Demonetization the QUANTUM JUMP
DIGITAL Economy Millennium OPPORTUNITY

Psychology
What is Psychology?: Unlocking Practical Tools for Growth
The 7-Figure Network
The Catalyst Code
The Potential Trap

Watch for more at https://drraam.com/.

Table of Contents

To every trailblazer who has stared into the fog of uncertainty and dared to take a step forward.

This book is for the leaders, dreamers, and restless problem-solvers who choose to turn chaos into clarity, disruption into direction, and adversity into advantage. May you never wait for certainty—but create it.

*"The future doesn't belong to those who predict it—it belongs to those who **catalyze** it."* – Dr. Raam Harvard

The Catalyst Code: How to Thrive in an Age of Uncertainty and Turn Chaos into Your Competitive Advantage.

INTRODUCTION : EMBRACING the Unknown

In an ever-changing world marked by rapid advancements, unforeseen challenges, and unprecedented complexities, the ability to navigate uncertainty has become a critical skill. The landscape of our personal and professional lives is fraught with ambiguity—whether it's the unpredictable nature of global markets, the constant evolution of technology, or the shifting dynamics of interpersonal relationships. As we grapple with these uncertainties, the question arises: how do we not only survive but thrive amidst chaos? The answer lies in embracing the unknown and recognizing the vital role that catalysts play in this transformative journey.

Overview of the Book's Purpose

The Catalyst Code: How to Thrive in an Age of Uncertainty and Turn Chaos into Your Competitive Advantage is designed to provide readers with a comprehensive framework for understanding and navigating uncertainty. This book serves as a guide for individuals seeking to cultivate resilience, adaptability, and innovation in their lives. It aims to equip readers with the mindset, tools, and strategies necessary to turn uncertainty into an opportunity for growth and transformation.

In exploring the nuances of uncertainty, we will delve into the psychological, emotional, and practical aspects that influence our ability to navigate the unknown. By shedding light on the common fears and anxieties associated with ambiguity, we aim to empower readers to confront their apprehensions head-on and harness their potential as catalysts for change.

The Significance of Navigating Uncertainty

The significance of navigating uncertainty cannot be overstated. In today's fast-paced world, change is not only inevitable; it is a constant force that shapes our realities. Whether we face economic downturns, technological disruptions, or personal crises, the ability to adapt and thrive in the face of the unknown is paramount. Those who can effectively navigate uncertainty are often better positioned to seize opportunities, foster innovation, and inspire others.

Navigating uncertainty also involves cultivating a deeper understanding of ourselves and the world around us. As we confront the unknown, we are often pushed to reevaluate our values, beliefs, and priorities. This process of self-discovery is not only essential for personal growth but also for forging meaningful connections with others. In essence, navigating uncertainty is about embracing change, taking calculated risks, and finding strength in vulnerability.

Introducing Catalysts: Essential Guides Through the Unknown

At the heart of this journey are catalysts—individuals who play a pivotal role in transforming uncertainty into opportunity. Catalysts are not merely passive observers; they are proactive agents of change who inspire and empower others to embrace the unknown. Whether in a personal or professional context, catalysts possess a unique mindset and skill set that enables them to navigate ambiguity with confidence and purpose.

Catalysts are characterized by their ability to foster collaboration, encourage innovative thinking, and build supportive networks. They are skilled at identifying opportunities within challenges, enabling them to drive progress even in the most turbulent times. By leveraging their strengths and experiences, catalysts create environments where others feel empowered to take risks, explore new ideas, and embrace uncertainty.

Throughout this book, we will explore the various dimensions of catalysts and how they can guide us through the unknown. From cultivating a catalyst mindset to building meaningful connections, we will provide practical strategies and insights to help readers embrace their roles as catalysts in their own lives.

The Journey Ahead

As we embark on this journey together, readers will discover that navigating uncertainty is not a solitary endeavor. It is a collective experience that thrives on collaboration, empathy, and shared learning. Each chapter of this book will build upon the last, providing readers with a comprehensive toolkit for navigating the unknown.

In the chapters that follow, we will delve deeper into the nature of uncertainty, explore the characteristics of effective catalysts, and provide actionable strategies for overcoming challenges. From decision-making frameworks to techniques for fostering innovation, each section will equip readers with the tools they need to thrive in an unpredictable world.

Ultimately, *The Catalyst Code: How to Thrive in an Age of Uncertainty and Turn Chaos into Your Competitive Advantage*is not just about surviving uncertainty; it is about thriving amidst it. By embracing the unknown and cultivating our roles as catalysts, we can unlock our potential and inspire transformative change in ourselves and others.

Conclusion

In conclusion, the journey of navigating uncertainty begins with a willingness to embrace the unknown. By understanding the significance of uncertainty and recognizing the role of catalysts, we can embark on a path of growth and transformation. As we move forward, let us commit to being catalysts in our own lives, guiding ourselves and others through the complexities of change. Together, we can unlock the power of uncertainty and create a future filled with possibility.

Chapter 1: The Nature of Uncertainty

Uncertainty is an inherent part of life, a constant companion in our personal and professional journeys. In a world characterized by rapid change, complexity, and unpredictability, understanding the nature of uncertainty is crucial for navigating it effectively. This chapter will explore the different facets of uncertainty, its impact on individuals and organizations, and the psychological effects it can have. Additionally, we will discuss strategies for managing these effects and embracing uncertainty as a catalyst for growth.

Understanding the Facets of Uncertainty

Uncertainty manifests in various forms, each with distinct implications. By categorizing these facets, we can gain a deeper understanding of how uncertainty operates and how it affects our lives.

1. Types of Uncertainty

a. Epistemic Uncertainty

Epistemic uncertainty arises from a lack of knowledge or information about a situation. It is prevalent in fields such as science, economics, and decision-making, where data may be incomplete or ambiguous. For instance, a company launching a new product may face epistemic uncertainty regarding market demand or consumer preferences. This type of uncertainty often leads to questions like, "What do we not know?" and "How can we fill these knowledge gaps?"

b. Aleatory Uncertainty

Aleatory uncertainty, also known as stochastic uncertainty, is inherent in the randomness and unpredictability of certain events. It is often encountered in situations governed by chance, such as natural disasters, economic fluctuations, and sports outcomes. For example, the unpredictable nature of the stock market reflects aleatory uncertainty, as various external factors can influence prices and trends.

c. Ontological Uncertainty

Ontological uncertainty refers to the unpredictability of complex systems and the limits of our understanding. It arises when we confront situations where outcomes are not just unknown but also fundamentally unpredictable due to the complexity of interactions. For instance, climate change presents ontological uncertainty because it involves multiple variables interacting in intricate ways, making it challenging to predict specific future scenarios.

2. The Impact of Uncertainty on Individuals

Uncertainty can significantly affect individuals, shaping their thoughts, emotions, and behaviors. Understanding these impacts is essential for developing effective coping strategies.

a. Emotional Responses

When faced with uncertainty, individuals often experience a range of emotions, including anxiety, fear, and stress. The fear of the unknown can lead to heightened anxiety levels, which may manifest as physical symptoms such as increased heart rate, sweating, or difficulty concentrating. Over time, chronic exposure to uncertainty can lead to mental health issues, including depression and burnout.

b. Decision-Making Challenges

Uncertainty complicates decision-making processes. Individuals may struggle to make choices when outcomes are uncertain, leading to paralysis by analysis. This phenomenon occurs when the fear of making the wrong decision prevents individuals from taking action. As a result, they may become stuck in indecision, missing opportunities for growth and progress.

c. Impact on Performance

Uncertainty can also affect performance in various domains, including work and personal life. For example, employees in organizations facing significant changes may experience decreased job satisfaction and productivity due to uncertainty about their roles and future prospects. Similarly, students navigating uncertain academic paths may struggle with motivation and engagement.

3. The Impact of Uncertainty on Organizations

Organizations are not immune to the effects of uncertainty, and understanding how it influences their operations is crucial for effective management.

a. Strategic Planning Challenges

Uncertainty poses significant challenges to strategic planning. Organizations must navigate changing market conditions, regulatory environments, and consumer preferences. For instance, during economic downturns, companies may face uncertainty regarding revenue forecasts and resource allocation. This unpredictability can hinder long-term planning and lead to reactive rather than proactive strategies.

b. Organizational Culture and Morale

Uncertainty can shape organizational culture and employee morale. In environments characterized by constant change, employees may feel insecure about their jobs, leading to decreased engagement and motivation. Conversely, organizations that foster a culture of adaptability and open communication can better navigate uncertainty and maintain employee morale.

c. Innovation and Risk-Taking

Uncertainty can either stifle or stimulate innovation. On one hand, fear of failure in uncertain environments may discourage risk-taking and creative thinking. On the other hand, organizations that embrace uncertainty as a catalyst for innovation can find new opportunities and solutions. For example, companies that invest in research and development often thrive by exploring uncharted territories.

The Psychological Effects of Uncertainty

Uncertainty can profoundly affect our psychological well-being. Understanding these effects is essential for developing strategies to manage uncertainty effectively.

1. Anxiety and Fear

The psychological effects of uncertainty often manifest as anxiety and fear. When faced with ambiguous situations, individuals may experience heightened stress levels, which can impact their mental health. Anxiety can lead to rumination, where individuals repeatedly think about potential negative outcomes, exacerbating their fears. This cycle can hinder their ability to take action and contribute to a sense of helplessness.

2. Cognitive Distortions

Uncertainty can lead to cognitive distortions, where individuals perceive situations inaccurately due to their fear of the unknown. For example, they may catastrophize potential outcomes, believing that the worst-case scenario is the most likely to occur. This negative thinking can create a feedback loop, reinforcing feelings of anxiety and hopelessness.

3. Resilience and Adaptability

On the flip side, navigating uncertainty can foster resilience and adaptability. When individuals confront and overcome challenges, they often develop a greater sense of self-efficacy and confidence in their abilities. Building resilience involves reframing uncertainty as an opportunity for growth and learning, allowing individuals to approach challenges with a positive mindset.

Strategies for Managing Uncertainty

While uncertainty can be daunting, there are strategies individuals and organizations can employ to manage its effects effectively.

1. Embracing a Growth Mindset

Cultivating a growth mindset is crucial for navigating uncertainty. A growth mindset emphasizes the belief that abilities and intelligence can be developed through effort and learning. When individuals adopt this mindset, they are more likely to view uncertainty as an opportunity for growth rather than a threat. They become more open to learning from failures and adapting their approaches.

2. Practicing Mindfulness

Mindfulness techniques can help individuals manage anxiety and stress associated with uncertainty. Mindfulness encourages individuals to stay present in the moment and observe their thoughts and feelings without judgment. By practicing mindfulness, individuals can develop a greater awareness of their emotional responses and reduce anxiety related to the unknown.

3. Setting Realistic Expectations

Setting realistic expectations can help individuals cope with uncertainty more effectively. By acknowledging that not everything is within their control, individuals can focus on what they can influence. This approach reduces the pressure to predict every outcome and encourages a more flexible mindset.

4. Building Supportive Networks

Establishing supportive networks is essential for navigating uncertainty. Connecting with others who share similar experiences can provide valuable perspectives and emotional support. Collaborative environments foster open communication and create a sense of community, enabling individuals to share challenges and find solutions together.

5. Developing Decision-Making Frameworks

Implementing structured decision-making frameworks can help individuals and organizations navigate uncertainty more effectively. By outlining clear criteria for decision-making, individuals can reduce ambiguity and make more informed choices. Frameworks such as the SWOT analysis (Strengths, Weaknesses, Opportunities, Threats) provide a systematic approach to evaluating options.

Conclusion

Uncertainty is an inherent part of the human experience, affecting individuals and organizations in profound ways. By understanding the different facets of uncertainty and its psychological effects, we can develop effective strategies for managing it. Embracing uncertainty as a catalyst for growth and transformation allows us to navigate the unknown with confidence and resilience. As we move forward in this book, we will explore practical tools and frameworks to help readers harness the power of uncertainty in their lives, ultimately transforming it into a pathway for success and innovation.

Chapter 2: Developing a Catalyst Mindset

In an era defined by rapid change and uncertainty, the ability to adapt and thrive is more crucial than ever. At the heart of this ability lies what we call the "catalyst mindset." This mindset encompasses a set of beliefs, attitudes, and behaviors that empower individuals to not only navigate change but to leverage it as an opportunity for growth and transformation. In this chapter, we will define the catalyst mindset, explore its importance in managing change, and offer practical strategies for cultivating resilience, adaptability, and a growth-oriented approach.

Defining the Catalyst Mindset

The catalyst mindset is a proactive and transformative way of thinking that positions individuals to effectively engage with change and uncertainty. Unlike a fixed mindset, which views challenges as threats, a catalyst mindset perceives obstacles as opportunities for learning and improvement.

1. Key Characteristics of the Catalyst Mindset

a. Curiosity

Curiosity is the cornerstone of the catalyst mindset. Individuals with a catalyst mindset approach the world with an open mind, eager to learn and explore new possibilities. They ask questions, seek diverse perspectives, and remain receptive to new ideas. This inquisitive nature enables them to identify opportunities within challenges.

b. Resilience

Resilience is the ability to bounce back from setbacks and maintain a positive outlook in the face of adversity. A catalyst mindset fosters resilience by encouraging individuals to view failures as stepping stones to success. Rather than being deterred by obstacles, they learn from their experiences and use them as fuel for growth.

c. Adaptability

Adaptability is the capacity to adjust to new circumstances and embrace change. Those with a catalyst mindset are not only willing to change but also thrive in dynamic environments. They recognize that change is a constant in life and are prepared to pivot when necessary, allowing them to navigate uncertainties with confidence.

d. Growth Orientation

A growth-oriented approach is fundamental to the catalyst mindset. Individuals who embrace this mindset believe that their abilities and intelligence can be developed through dedication and hard work. They see challenges as opportunities for growth rather than threats, fostering a lifelong learning attitude.

2. Importance of the Catalyst Mindset in Navigating Change

The catalyst mindset is essential for thriving in today's rapidly changing world. Here are several reasons why cultivating this mindset is crucial:

a. Enhanced Problem-Solving Skills

A catalyst mindset empowers individuals to tackle problems creatively and effectively. By viewing challenges as opportunities, individuals can think outside the box and develop innovative solutions. This approach is particularly valuable in uncertain environments where traditional methods may fall short.

b. Increased Confidence

When individuals adopt a catalyst mindset, they develop a greater sense of self-efficacy—the belief in their ability to succeed in specific situations. This confidence enables them to take calculated risks, pursue new opportunities, and step out of their comfort zones, ultimately leading to personal and professional growth.

c. Stronger Relationships

Individuals with a catalyst mindset tend to cultivate positive relationships with others. Their openness to learning and collaboration fosters trust and connection, enabling them to build strong networks of support. This sense of community is essential for navigating change, as it provides emotional and practical resources during challenging times.

d. Sustainable Motivation

A catalyst mindset promotes intrinsic motivation, the drive that comes from within. By focusing on growth and learning, individuals find motivation in the process itself, rather than solely in outcomes. This sustainable motivation allows them to persevere through challenges and maintain momentum even when faced with setbacks.

Strategies for Cultivating a Catalyst Mindset

While the catalyst mindset may come naturally to some, it can also be cultivated through intentional practice. In this section, we will explore practical strategies for developing resilience, adaptability, and a growth-oriented approach.

1. Foster Curiosity

a. Embrace Lifelong Learning

Cultivating a catalyst mindset begins with a commitment to lifelong learning. Seek out opportunities for education, whether through formal courses, workshops, or self-directed study. Explore topics that interest you, and remain open to new ideas and perspectives.

b. Ask Questions

Adopt a habit of inquiry by asking questions about your surroundings, experiences, and beliefs. Encourage yourself to think critically and seek deeper understanding. Questions like "What can I learn from this experience?" and "How might I approach this differently?" can stimulate curiosity and promote exploration.

c. Engage in Diverse Experiences

Expose yourself to diverse experiences, cultures, and perspectives. Travel, volunteer, or participate in community events to broaden your horizons. Engaging with people from different backgrounds can ignite your curiosity and inspire new ways of thinking.

2. Build Resilience

a. Reframe Failures

To cultivate resilience, learn to reframe failures as opportunities for growth. Instead of viewing setbacks as personal shortcomings, consider what you can learn from them. Ask yourself, "What went wrong?" and "How can I improve next time?" This reflective practice helps you develop a growth-oriented mindset.

b. Practice Self-Compassion

Be kind to yourself during challenging times. Acknowledge that everyone faces setbacks and that failure is a natural part of the learning process. Practicing self-compassion allows you to bounce back more quickly from disappointments and maintain a positive outlook.

c. Develop Coping Strategies

Identify and develop coping strategies that work for you. These might include mindfulness practices, journaling, or engaging in physical activity. Having a toolbox of coping mechanisms can help you navigate stress and adversity more effectively.

3. Embrace Adaptability

a. Stay Flexible

Embrace flexibility in your plans and goals. Understand that change is inevitable and that adapting to new circumstances is a sign of strength. When faced with unexpected challenges, practice pivoting your approach and being open to alternative solutions.

b. Cultivate a Problem-Solving Mindset

Develop a proactive problem-solving mindset. When confronted with challenges, focus on finding solutions rather than dwelling on the problems. Break down obstacles into manageable steps and explore various options to overcome them.

c. Learn to Let Go of Control

Recognize that not everything is within your control. Learning to let go of the need to control outcomes can alleviate stress and open you up to new possibilities. Focus on what you can influence and be willing to adapt to external factors.

4. Nurture a Growth-Oriented Approach

a. Set Growth-Oriented Goals

Instead of setting goals solely focused on outcomes, incorporate growth-oriented goals into your planning. For example, aim to develop specific skills or knowledge rather than simply achieving a particular result. This approach encourages you to prioritize the learning process.

b. Seek Feedback

Actively seek feedback from others to foster growth. Constructive criticism provides valuable insights into your strengths and areas for improvement. Embrace feedback as an opportunity to learn and develop, rather than viewing it as a threat to your self-esteem.

c. Celebrate Progress

Acknowledge and celebrate your progress, no matter how small. Recognizing your achievements reinforces a growth-oriented mindset and motivates you to continue striving for improvement. Take time to reflect on your journey and appreciate the steps you've taken along the way.

Conclusion

The catalyst mindset is a powerful framework for navigating change and uncertainty. By cultivating curiosity, resilience, adaptability, and a growth-oriented approach, individuals can thrive in the face of challenges and harness change as a catalyst for transformation. In the chapters that follow, we will explore practical tools and strategies to further develop the catalyst mindset, empowering readers to embrace their roles as agents of change in their own lives and communities.

Chapter 3: Navigational Tools for Decision-Making

In the landscape of uncertainty, effective decision-making becomes a vital skill for individuals and organizations alike. The ability to assess risks, evaluate options, and make informed choices can determine the course of one's journey through the unknown. This chapter presents frameworks and tools designed to aid decision-making, emphasizing techniques such as scenario planning and risk analysis. By equipping readers with these navigational tools, we empower them to approach decision-making with confidence and clarity, ultimately transforming challenges into opportunities.

Understanding Decision-Making in Uncertainty

Before delving into specific tools and frameworks, it's essential to understand the nature of decision-making, especially in contexts characterized by uncertainty.

1. The Nature of Decision-Making

Decision-making involves selecting a course of action from multiple alternatives based on available information and desired outcomes. In uncertain environments, the complexity of decisions increases, requiring individuals to account for various factors, including incomplete information, unpredictable variables, and potential risks.

2. The Role of Cognitive Biases

Cognitive biases can significantly impact decision-making. These mental shortcuts or errors in judgment can lead to irrational choices, especially under pressure. Awareness of common biases—such as confirmation bias, anchoring, and overconfidence—can help individuals mitigate their effects and enhance the quality of their decisions.

Frameworks for Effective Decision-Making

To navigate the complexities of decision-making, several frameworks can provide structure and clarity. This section explores key decision-making frameworks, offering practical insights into their application.

1. The DECIDE Framework

The DECIDE framework is a step-by-step process that guides individuals through the decision-making journey. Each letter represents a key component of effective decision-making:

- **D - Define the problem:** Clearly articulate the issue at hand, ensuring a thorough understanding of its context and implications.
- **E - Establish criteria:** Determine the criteria for evaluating options, such as cost, feasibility, and alignment with values.
- **C - Consider alternatives:** Brainstorm a range of potential solutions or courses of action, avoiding premature judgment of their viability.
- **I - Identify the best alternative:** Evaluate each alternative against the established criteria and select the most suitable option.
- **D - Develop and implement an action plan:** Create a detailed plan outlining the steps necessary to execute the chosen alternative.
- **E - Evaluate the decision:** After implementation, assess the

outcomes and learn from the experience to inform future decisions.

2. The SWOT Analysis

SWOT analysis is a widely used framework for assessing the strengths, weaknesses, opportunities, and threats associated with a particular decision or situation. It involves:

- **Strengths:** Identify the internal strengths that can support the decision.
- **Weaknesses:** Recognize the internal weaknesses that may hinder success.
- **Opportunities:** Explore external opportunities that could be leveraged.
- **Threats:** Acknowledge external threats that could pose challenges.

By analyzing these four dimensions, individuals can gain a comprehensive understanding of the factors influencing their decision and develop strategies to maximize strengths while mitigating weaknesses.

3. The Cost-Benefit Analysis

Cost-benefit analysis is a quantitative method for evaluating the potential benefits and costs associated with a decision. The process involves:

- **Identifying costs:** Enumerate all costs, including direct, indirect, and opportunity costs.
- **Identifying benefits:** Estimate the potential benefits, both tangible and intangible, resulting from the decision.
- **Comparing costs and benefits:** Calculate the net benefit by subtracting total costs from total benefits. A positive net

benefit suggests a favorable decision.

This analytical approach provides a clear framework for weighing options and making informed choices based on economic viability.

Navigational Tools for Risk Assessment

Understanding and assessing risks is a critical component of effective decision-making, particularly in uncertain environments. This section explores essential tools and techniques for evaluating risks.

1. Risk Analysis

Risk analysis involves identifying, assessing, and prioritizing risks associated with a decision or project. The process typically includes:

a. Risk Identification

Identify potential risks that may impact the decision. This can involve brainstorming sessions, expert consultations, and historical data analysis.

b. Risk Assessment

Evaluate the likelihood and impact of each identified risk. This can be achieved through qualitative methods (e.g., expert judgment) or quantitative methods (e.g., statistical analysis).

c. Risk Prioritization

Rank risks based on their significance to the decision. This prioritization helps focus resources on the most critical risks, enabling effective management strategies.

2. Scenario Planning

Scenario planning is a strategic method for exploring and preparing for potential future scenarios. This technique involves:

a. Identifying Key Drivers

Determine the key factors that could influence the future landscape, such as technological advancements, market trends, or regulatory changes.

b. Developing Scenarios

Create a set of diverse scenarios based on different combinations of key drivers. Each scenario should represent a plausible future state, allowing for exploration of various possibilities.

c. Analyzing Implications

Evaluate the implications of each scenario for decision-making. Consider how different choices may lead to distinct outcomes in each scenario, enabling better preparedness for uncertainty.

3. Decision Trees

Decision trees are visual representations of decision-making processes that map out options, outcomes, and associated risks. The process involves:

- **Identifying Decision Points:** Begin by outlining the initial decision and branching out to represent different options.
- **Estimating Outcomes:** For each option, estimate potential outcomes and their probabilities.
- **Calculating Expected Values:** Assign values to outcomes and calculate the expected value for each option by multiplying the outcome value by its probability.

Decision trees provide a clear visual framework for analyzing complex decisions and their potential consequences, helping individuals make more informed choices.

Techniques for Enhancing Decision-Making

Beyond frameworks and tools, several techniques can enhance the decision-making process, enabling individuals to navigate uncertainty effectively.

1. Embracing Collaborative Decision-Making

Collaborative decision-making involves engaging diverse perspectives and expertise in the decision-making process. This approach fosters creativity, reduces biases, and enhances the quality of decisions. Techniques include:

- **Brainstorming Sessions:** Facilitate open discussions to generate ideas and explore various viewpoints.
- **Focus Groups:** Gather input from a representative group to gain insights into preferences and concerns.

2. Utilizing Technology for Data Analysis

In today's digital age, technology can play a pivotal role in enhancing decision-making. Data analysis tools and software can help individuals make sense of complex information, identify trends, and assess risks. Consider leveraging:

- **Business Intelligence Tools:** Use software that aggregates and analyzes data to inform decision-making.
- **Predictive Analytics:** Employ algorithms to forecast potential outcomes based on historical data and trends.

3. Developing Intuition and Emotional Intelligence

While analytical tools are essential, decision-making also involves intuition and emotional intelligence. Cultivating these qualities can enhance decision-making in uncertain environments:

- **Reflective Practices:** Encourage self-reflection to better understand personal values, biases, and instincts.
- **Emotional Awareness:** Develop emotional intelligence by recognizing and managing emotions in yourself and others, facilitating better interpersonal decision-making.

Case Studies of Effective Decision-Making

To illustrate the application of navigational tools for decision-making, this section presents case studies of individuals and organizations that have successfully navigated uncertainty through effective decision-making processes.

1. Case Study: Procter & Gamble's Scenario Planning

Procter & Gamble (P&G) is renowned for its strategic use of scenario planning. Faced with a rapidly changing consumer landscape, P&G developed multiple scenarios exploring various market conditions, consumer behaviors, and competitive dynamics. By preparing for different futures, the company was able to adapt its marketing strategies and product offerings, ultimately leading to increased market share and customer loyalty.

2. Case Study: NASA's Risk Analysis in Space Missions

NASA employs rigorous risk analysis methodologies to ensure the safety and success of its space missions. By systematically identifying and assessing risks associated with different mission components, NASA can make informed decisions regarding launch schedules, mission parameters, and contingency plans. This analytical approach has contributed to numerous successful missions and advancements in space exploration.

3. Case Study: Airbnb's Collaborative Decision-Making

Airbnb exemplifies the power of collaborative decision-making in navigating challenges. When faced with the COVID-19 pandemic, the company engaged its global community of hosts and guests to gather insights and feedback on safety measures. By involving stakeholders in the decision-making process, Airbnb was able to develop effective policies that prioritized health and safety while maintaining trust within its community.

Conclusion

In an era defined by uncertainty, effective decision-making is a crucial navigational skill. By employing frameworks such as DECIDE, SWOT analysis, and cost-benefit analysis, individuals can systematically approach decision-making, enhancing their ability to evaluate options and assess risks. Additionally, tools like risk analysis, scenario planning, and decision trees provide valuable insights into navigating complexity. By embracing collaborative decision-making, leveraging technology, and cultivating intuition, readers can further enhance their decision-making capabilities. As they journey through the unknown, these navigational tools will empower them to make informed choices, turning uncertainty into opportunity.

Chapter 4: Building a Supportive Network

In times of uncertainty, the strength and support of a network can make all the difference in an individual's ability to navigate challenges. This chapter highlights the crucial role of collaboration and relationships in overcoming adversity, emphasizing that a supportive network is not merely a safety net but a catalyst for growth and resilience. We will explore strategies for fostering diverse and supportive networks, enabling readers to build connections that empower them in their journey through the unknown.

The Importance of Supportive Networks in Uncertainty

1. Defining Supportive Networks

Supportive networks encompass a range of relationships, including friends, family, colleagues, mentors, and acquaintances. These connections can provide emotional support, practical resources, and valuable insights that are essential when facing uncertainty. Supportive networks are characterized by trust, mutual respect, and open communication, allowing individuals to share their challenges and seek guidance.

2. The Psychological Benefits of Support

Research shows that having a strong support network can significantly impact psychological well-being. During uncertain times, social support can buffer against stress, anxiety, and feelings of isolation. Supportive relationships contribute to:

- **Emotional Resilience:** Knowing that others are available to help can foster a sense of security and confidence.
- **Reduced Anxiety:** Engaging with a support network can alleviate feelings of fear and uncertainty, providing perspective and reassurance.
- **Enhanced Problem-Solving:** Collaborative relationships can lead to diverse insights and solutions, making it easier to navigate complex situations.

The Role of Collaboration in Navigating Uncertainty

Collaboration is a cornerstone of effective networking, especially in uncertain environments. This section explores how collaboration enhances the ability to navigate challenges and fosters a sense of community.

1. Sharing Knowledge and Resources

One of the most significant advantages of collaboration is the pooling of knowledge and resources. When individuals come together to share their expertise and experiences, they can uncover new solutions and strategies for overcoming obstacles. Collaborative environments encourage:

- **Idea Generation:** Group discussions often lead to creative solutions that individuals may not have considered independently.
- **Resource Sharing:** Networks can facilitate access to resources, tools, and support that may not be available individually.

2. Building Collective Resilience

Collective resilience is the ability of a group to withstand challenges and bounce back from adversity. In a supportive network, individuals can rely on one another to navigate uncertainty more effectively. This can involve:

- **Mutual Encouragement:** Supporting one another through difficult times can enhance motivation and accountability.
- **Collective Problem-Solving:** A group can approach problems from multiple angles, increasing the likelihood of finding effective solutions.

Strategies for Building a Supportive Network

To cultivate a supportive network that empowers individuals to navigate uncertainty, the following strategies can be employed:

1. Identify Your Network's Purpose

Before expanding or nurturing a network, it's crucial to define its purpose. Understanding what you hope to achieve through your connections will guide your networking efforts. Consider:

- **Professional Development:** Are you looking to enhance your skills or advance your career?
- **Emotional Support:** Do you seek companionship and understanding during difficult times?
- **Knowledge Sharing:** Are you interested in exchanging ideas and insights with others?

2. Diversify Your Connections

A diverse network brings together individuals from different backgrounds, experiences, and perspectives. This diversity enriches conversations and fosters creativity. Strategies for diversifying connections include:

- **Engaging with Different Communities:** Attend events, workshops, or groups that attract people outside your usual circle. This can include professional conferences, community gatherings, or social clubs.
- **Utilizing Social Media:** Platforms like LinkedIn, Twitter, and Facebook can help you connect with individuals from various fields and locations. Engage in discussions and follow thought leaders to broaden your network.

3. Cultivate Authentic Relationships

Building authentic relationships requires effort and intentionality. The following practices can help foster genuine connections:

- **Active Listening:** Show genuine interest in others by listening attentively and asking thoughtful questions. This demonstrates that you value their perspectives and experiences.
- **Be Vulnerable:** Sharing your challenges and experiences can encourage others to do the same, creating an environment of trust and openness.
- **Follow Up:** After meeting someone, follow up with a personalized message or invite them for coffee. This reinforces the connection and shows your commitment to building the relationship.

4. Create Opportunities for Collaboration

Collaboration can be fostered through intentional actions that encourage group engagement. Consider the following:

- **Organize Group Activities:** Host workshops, brainstorming sessions, or networking events that encourage collaboration among your connections. This can strengthen relationships and lead to shared insights.

- **Establish Accountability Partnerships:** Pair up with someone who shares similar goals and check in regularly to discuss progress, challenges, and strategies for moving forward.

5. Nurture Your Network Over Time

Building a supportive network is an ongoing process that requires maintenance. The following strategies can help sustain relationships:

- **Regular Check-Ins:** Schedule regular touchpoints with your connections to maintain engagement. This can be as simple as sending a message to ask how they're doing or sharing relevant articles.
- **Celebrate Achievements:** Acknowledge the milestones and successes of your network members. Celebrating achievements fosters a positive atmosphere and strengthens relationships.
- **Provide Support:** Offer your assistance when connections face challenges. This can involve sharing resources, providing advice, or simply being there to listen.

6. Leverage Technology for Connection

In today's digital age, technology plays a vital role in building and maintaining networks. Utilize various tools and platforms to enhance connectivity:

- **Networking Apps:** Explore applications designed for networking, such as Meetup or Bumble Bizz, to connect with individuals who share your interests or goals.
- **Virtual Events:** Attend webinars, online workshops, or virtual conferences to engage with a broader audience and foster new

connections.

Overcoming Barriers to Building Supportive Networks

While building a supportive network is valuable, individuals may encounter barriers that hinder their efforts. Understanding and addressing these obstacles is essential for fostering connections.

1. Fear of Rejection

Fear of rejection can prevent individuals from reaching out and building new connections. To overcome this fear:

- **Reframe Rejection:** Understand that rejection is a natural part of networking and does not reflect your worth. Focus on the connections you can create rather than those that don't materialize.
- **Start Small:** Begin by reaching out to acquaintances or individuals within your existing network to build confidence before approaching new connections.

2. Time Constraints

Busy schedules can limit the time available for networking. To address this challenge:

- **Prioritize Networking:** Treat networking as a priority by scheduling specific time slots for connecting with others. Even small, consistent efforts can lead to meaningful relationships.
- **Combine Activities:** Integrate networking into your existing commitments, such as attending events related to your hobbies or professional interests.

3. Imposter Syndrome

Many individuals struggle with feelings of inadequacy, leading them to doubt their ability to connect with others. To combat imposter syndrome:

- **Acknowledge Your Value:** Recognize your unique skills, experiences, and perspectives that contribute to your network. Embrace your individuality and the value you bring to connections.
- **Seek Support:** Connect with others who may share similar feelings. Engaging with individuals facing similar challenges can create a sense of community and reassurance.

Case Studies: Successful Supportive Networks

To illustrate the power of supportive networks in navigating uncertainty, this section highlights case studies of individuals and organizations that have successfully built and leveraged their networks.

1. Case Study: The Founders of Slack

The founders of Slack, Stewart Butterfield and his team, illustrate the importance of building a supportive network in the tech industry. Initially, the team faced numerous challenges during their startup phase. However, by cultivating relationships with other tech entrepreneurs and mentors, they were able to gain insights, share experiences, and ultimately create a platform that transformed workplace communication. Their collaborative approach not only strengthened their product but also built a strong network of advocates and supporters.

2. Case Study: Women in Tech Organizations

Organizations such as Women Who Code and Girls Who Code have successfully built supportive networks for women in the tech industry. By fostering diverse connections, these organizations provide mentorship, resources, and opportunities for women to collaborate, share knowledge, and support one another. This sense of community has empowered countless women to navigate the challenges of the tech industry, leading to increased representation and success.

3. Case Study: Local Business Networks

Local chambers of commerce and business associations serve as examples of supportive networks for entrepreneurs. These organizations provide a platform for local business owners to connect, collaborate, and share resources. During economic uncertainty, these networks have proven invaluable in helping businesses adapt, share best practices, and access resources that promote resilience and growth.

Conclusion

Building a supportive network is a critical aspect of navigating uncertainty. By fostering collaboration and relationships, individuals can create a safety net that empowers them to overcome challenges and seize opportunities. The strategies outlined in this chapter emphasize the importance of diversifying connections, cultivating authentic relationships, and nurturing networks over time. As readers take proactive steps to build their networks, they will find themselves better equipped to face the unknown, drawing strength and support from the connections they create. In the journey through uncertainty, a supportive network becomes an invaluable catalyst for growth, resilience, and transformation.

Chapter 5: Creative Problem-Solving in the Unknown

Navigating the unknown often requires more than traditional problem-solving methods; it demands creativity, adaptability, and innovative thinking. In this chapter, we will explore various approaches to creative problem-solving in ambiguous situations. By understanding and applying techniques such as design thinking and brainstorming, readers will be empowered to tackle challenges with a fresh perspective, turning uncertainty into opportunity.

Understanding Creative Problem-Solving

Creative problem-solving involves approaching challenges with an open mind and a willingness to explore unconventional solutions. Unlike traditional problem-solving, which often relies on established methodologies and linear processes, creative problem-solving emphasizes flexibility, exploration, and experimentation. This approach encourages individuals to think outside the box and consider multiple perspectives, leading to more innovative and effective solutions.

1. The Need for Creative Problem-Solving in Uncertainty

When faced with ambiguity, individuals may feel overwhelmed or unsure of how to proceed. Creative problem-solving can provide a framework for navigating these challenges, offering several benefits:

- **Enhanced Resilience:** Creative thinking fosters resilience by encouraging individuals to adapt and adjust their approaches as new information emerges.
- **Increased Engagement:** Innovative problem-solving techniques can engage team members and stakeholders, fostering collaboration and investment in the solutions developed.
- **Diverse Solutions:** By exploring a range of ideas and approaches, creative problem-solving can lead to unique solutions that may not have been considered through conventional methods.

Techniques for Creative Problem-Solving

This section will delve into specific techniques and methodologies that can facilitate creative problem-solving in the face of uncertainty.

1. Design Thinking

Design thinking is a human-centered approach to problem-solving that emphasizes empathy, collaboration, and experimentation. It involves a series of iterative steps that guide individuals and teams through the problem-solving process. The key phases of design thinking include:

a. Empathize

Understanding the needs and experiences of those affected by the problem is crucial. Empathy involves engaging with stakeholders, conducting interviews, and observing behaviors to gain insights into their perspectives. By deeply understanding the challenges faced by users, problem-solvers can identify root causes and areas for improvement.

b. Define

Once insights are gathered, the next step is to define the problem clearly. This involves synthesizing the information collected during the empathize phase to articulate a specific problem statement. A well-defined problem statement serves as a guiding light for the subsequent phases of the design thinking process.

c. Ideate

The ideation phase encourages brainstorming and the generation of a wide range of ideas. This is a critical step in creative problem-solving, as it allows participants to explore possibilities without judgment. Techniques for ideation include:

- **Brainstorming:** A free-flowing session where participants share ideas without critique, allowing creativity to flourish.
- **Mind Mapping:** A visual tool that helps organize thoughts and connections, making it easier to see relationships between ideas.

d. Prototype

In this phase, participants create tangible representations of their ideas. Prototyping allows individuals to experiment with concepts and test their viability. Prototypes can be low-fidelity (simple sketches or models) or high-fidelity (functional versions of a product). The goal is to quickly iterate and refine ideas based on feedback.

e. Test

Testing prototypes with users provides valuable insights and feedback. This phase encourages a willingness to learn from failures and adjust solutions based on real-world responses. The feedback gathered during testing informs further iterations, enhancing the final solution's effectiveness.

2. Brainstorming

Brainstorming is a widely recognized technique for generating creative ideas and solutions. It can be conducted in group settings or individually and encourages participants to share their thoughts without fear of criticism. Key principles for effective brainstorming include:

a. Set Clear Objectives

Before a brainstorming session, establish clear objectives and guidelines. Define the problem to be solved and the desired outcomes. This helps participants stay focused and ensures that the session is productive.

b. Create a Safe Environment

Fostering a supportive atmosphere is essential for effective brainstorming. Encourage participants to share their ideas freely and reassure them that all contributions are valuable. Avoid criticism or judgment during the idea generation phase to create a space where creativity can thrive.

c. Encourage Wild Ideas

Encourage participants to think outside the box and propose unconventional solutions. Often, the most innovative ideas emerge from seemingly outrageous suggestions. Remind participants that all ideas are valid during brainstorming.

d. Build on Each Other's Ideas

Encourage participants to listen actively and build upon each other's ideas. This collaborative approach can lead to unexpected combinations and enhance the creativity of the group.

e. Prioritize and Refine Ideas

After generating a list of ideas, review and prioritize them based on feasibility, impact, and alignment with the objectives. This process helps identify the most promising solutions for further exploration and development.

3. SCAMPER Technique

The SCAMPER technique is a creative thinking tool that encourages individuals to think critically about existing ideas or products by applying seven prompts:

- **Substitute:** What elements can be replaced or swapped?
- **Combine:** How can different ideas or concepts be integrated?
- **Adapt:** What modifications can be made to suit new contexts?

- **Modify:** What changes can enhance functionality or appeal?
- **Put to another use:** How can the idea or product serve a different purpose?
- **Eliminate:** What can be removed to simplify or improve?
- **Reverse:** What would happen if the process or order were inverted?

By systematically applying the SCAMPER prompts, individuals can explore new dimensions of existing ideas and discover innovative solutions.

4. Mindfulness and Creative Thinking

Incorporating mindfulness practices can enhance creative problem-solving. Mindfulness encourages individuals to focus on the present moment and cultivate awareness of their thoughts and feelings. This heightened awareness can lead to:

- **Reduced Stress:** Mindfulness can alleviate anxiety and stress, allowing individuals to approach problems with a clearer mind.
- **Increased Creativity:** By fostering an open mindset, mindfulness can enhance divergent thinking and encourage exploration of new ideas.

Techniques such as meditation, deep breathing, and reflective journaling can be integrated into the creative problem-solving process to promote mindfulness.

Overcoming Barriers to Creative Problem-Solving

While creative problem-solving offers numerous benefits, individuals may encounter barriers that hinder their ability to think creatively. This section explores common obstacles and strategies to overcome them.

1. Fear of Failure

Fear of failure can stifle creativity and prevent individuals from exploring new ideas. To combat this fear:

- **Reframe Failure:** Shift the perception of failure from a negative outcome to a valuable learning experience. Emphasize that each setback provides an opportunity for growth and improvement.
- **Encourage Experimentation:** Foster a culture that values experimentation and risk-taking. Highlight success stories that resulted from initial failures to inspire confidence.

2. Fixed Mindset

Individuals with a fixed mindset may believe that their abilities and intelligence are static, limiting their willingness to engage in creative problem-solving. To cultivate a growth mindset:

- **Emphasize Learning:** Encourage individuals to view challenges as opportunities to learn and grow. Celebrate effort and perseverance rather than solely focusing on outcomes.
- **Promote Curiosity:** Foster curiosity by encouraging individuals to ask questions, explore new ideas, and seek diverse perspectives.

3. Lack of Resources

Limited resources, whether financial, time-related, or personnel-based, can hinder creative problem-solving. To overcome this challenge:

- **Leverage Existing Assets:** Encourage individuals to identify and utilize available resources creatively. This may involve repurposing existing tools or seeking innovative partnerships.

- **Seek External Support:** Collaborate with external partners, organizations, or mentors who can provide additional resources, insights, or guidance.

4. Groupthink

In team settings, groupthink can stifle creativity as individuals may conform to prevailing opinions or avoid expressing dissenting views. To counteract groupthink:

- **Encourage Diverse Perspectives:** Actively seek input from individuals with different backgrounds, experiences, and viewpoints. Emphasize the value of diverse opinions in enhancing creativity.
- **Facilitate Open Discussions:** Create an environment where team members feel comfortable expressing differing opinions. Encourage constructive debate and critical thinking.

Case Studies: Creative Problem-Solving in Action

This section presents case studies that illustrate successful creative problem-solving in the face of uncertainty.

1. Case Study: Airbnb

When Airbnb first launched, it faced skepticism and challenges in gaining traction. The founders used creative problem-solving techniques to address obstacles, including:

- **User-Centric Design Thinking:** By empathizing with users' needs, Airbnb refined its platform and offerings based on feedback from both hosts and guests.
- **Innovative Marketing Strategies:** The founders leveraged creative marketing campaigns, including partnerships with

local artists, to promote their platform and attract users.

As a result, Airbnb transformed the travel industry and became a leader in the sharing economy, demonstrating the power of creative problem-solving.

2. Case Study: IDEO and the Design of the Palm V

IDEO, a design consultancy, used design thinking principles to create the Palm V, a groundbreaking handheld device. Their approach included:

- **Empathizing with Users:** IDEO conducted extensive research to understand user preferences and pain points.
- **Rapid Prototyping:** The team created multiple prototypes, iterating based on user feedback until they arrived at a refined final product.

The success of the Palm V showcased the effectiveness of creative problem-solving and design thinking in developing innovative products.

3. Case Study: NASA's Mars Rover

NASA's Mars Rover project exemplifies creative problem-solving in the face of uncertainty. Faced with the challenges of designing a vehicle capable of exploring the Martian surface, the team employed various strategies:

- **Collaborative Networks:** NASA brought together experts from diverse fields, including robotics, engineering, and geology, to collaborate on the project.
- **Iterative Prototyping:** The team created and tested multiple prototypes, allowing them to learn and adapt their designs based on real-world conditions.

Chapter 6: Case Studies of Successful Navigation

Navigating uncertainty is a skill that can significantly impact individuals and organizations, especially in today's rapidly changing world. This chapter will explore various real-world examples of people and organizations that have effectively maneuvered through challenging situations. By analyzing these case studies, we can extract valuable lessons and actionable insights that readers can apply to their own journeys through uncertainty.

Overview of Case Studies

The case studies presented in this chapter will cover a range of sectors, including business, technology, healthcare, and personal development. Each case study will provide an in-depth analysis of how the subjects successfully navigated uncertainty, focusing on their strategies, decision-making processes, and the impact of their actions.

Case Study 1: Apple Inc. – Innovation Amidst Market Challenges

Background

Apple Inc. is known for its innovative products and strong brand loyalty. However, the company has faced numerous challenges, particularly during the late 1990s when it struggled to maintain market share against competitors like Microsoft and Dell.

Navigation Strategies

1. **Embracing Innovation**: Under the leadership of Steve Jobs, Apple pivoted towards innovation, focusing on developing unique products that combined functionality and design. The introduction of the iMac in 1998 marked a significant turnaround for the company.
2. **Customer-Centric Approach**: Apple placed a strong emphasis on understanding customer needs and preferences. This insight drove the design of the iPod, iPhone, and iPad, products that transformed consumer electronics.
3. **Strong Brand Identity**: Apple cultivated a distinctive brand identity that resonated with consumers. This branding strategy helped differentiate its products in a crowded marketplace.

Lessons Learned

- **Adaptability is Key**: Companies must be willing to pivot and adapt their strategies in response to market changes and customer feedback.
- **Innovative Culture**: Fostering a culture of innovation can lead to breakthroughs that redefine industries.
- **Customer Engagement**: Understanding and engaging with customers can drive product development and enhance brand loyalty.

Case Study 2: Johnson & Johnson – Crisis Management During the Tylenol Incident

Background

In 1982, Johnson & Johnson faced a major crisis when several people died after ingesting cyanide-laced Tylenol capsules in the Chicago area.

This incident posed a significant threat to the company's reputation and market share.

Navigation Strategies

1. **Transparent Communication**: Johnson & Johnson immediately issued a nationwide recall of Tylenol products, prioritizing consumer safety over profits. The company communicated openly with the media and the public about the situation.
2. **Swift Action**: The company acted quickly to develop tamper-proof packaging, restoring consumer confidence in its products. This innovation set new industry standards for product safety.
3. **Rebuilding Trust**: Through proactive public relations efforts and a focus on transparency, Johnson & Johnson successfully rebuilt its brand reputation.

Lessons Learned

- **Prioritize Safety**: In times of crisis, prioritize the safety and well-being of consumers above all else.
- **Effective Communication**: Transparent communication can mitigate damage and foster trust during crises.
- **Innovation in Response to Challenges**: Developing new solutions in response to crises can not only restore confidence but also position a company as a leader in its industry.

Case Study 3: Airbnb – Adapting to a Global Pandemic

Background

Airbnb faced significant challenges during the COVID-19 pandemic as travel restrictions led to a dramatic decline in bookings. The company had to navigate a landscape of uncertainty while prioritizing the safety of its hosts and guests.

Navigation Strategies

1. **Flexible Policies**: Airbnb implemented flexible cancellation policies to accommodate travelers' changing plans, demonstrating empathy and responsiveness to customer needs.
2. **Focus on Local Experiences**: To adapt to the new reality, Airbnb pivoted towards promoting local stays and experiences, encouraging users to explore their own cities.
3. **Health and Safety Protocols**: The company introduced enhanced cleaning protocols for hosts, ensuring the safety of guests and boosting confidence in the platform.

Lessons Learned

- **Flexibility is Essential**: Being flexible and responsive to customer needs can help businesses navigate uncertain times effectively.
- **Adapt to Changing Markets**: Understanding market trends and shifting consumer behavior is crucial for sustained success.
- **Prioritize Safety and Trust**: Implementing safety measures can help build trust and encourage customer engagement.

Case Study 4: Tesla – Disrupting the Automotive Industry

Background

Tesla, founded by Elon Musk, aimed to disrupt the traditional automotive industry by producing electric vehicles (EVs). The company faced significant uncertainty and skepticism in its early years due to the challenges of scaling production and competing against established automakers.

Navigation Strategies

1. **Visionary Leadership**: Elon Musk's visionary leadership and commitment to sustainability drove Tesla's mission and inspired employees to overcome challenges.
2. **Continuous Innovation**: Tesla continually invested in research and development, leading to advancements in battery technology and autonomous driving capabilities.
3. **Building a Supportive Community**: Tesla fostered a passionate community of supporters who advocated for the brand, helping to establish a strong market presence.

Lessons Learned

- **Vision and Commitment**: A clear vision can motivate teams and attract support even in uncertain times.
- **Invest in Innovation**: Continuous innovation is crucial for staying ahead in a rapidly evolving market.
- **Community Engagement**: Building a supportive community can enhance brand loyalty and drive success.

Case Study 5: Starbucks – Adapting to Changing Consumer Preferences

Background

Starbucks, the global coffeehouse chain, faced significant challenges in adapting to changing consumer preferences and economic downturns. The company needed to innovate to maintain its market position.

Navigation Strategies

1. **Product Diversification**: Starbucks expanded its menu to include a variety of beverages and food options, catering to diverse customer tastes and dietary preferences.
2. **Embracing Technology**: The company embraced technology by launching a mobile app for ordering and payments, enhancing customer convenience and engagement.
3. **Focus on Social Responsibility**: Starbucks committed to social responsibility initiatives, such as sourcing ethical coffee and supporting local communities, which resonated with consumers.

Lessons Learned

- **Stay Relevant**: Continuously innovating and diversifying offerings is essential for staying relevant in a competitive market.
- **Embrace Technology**: Leveraging technology can enhance customer experience and operational efficiency.
- **Align with Consumer Values**: Understanding and aligning with consumer values can strengthen brand loyalty and engagement.

Conclusion: Synthesizing Insights for Effective Navigation

The case studies presented in this chapter highlight various strategies and approaches that individuals and organizations have used to successfully navigate uncertainty. By analyzing these real-world examples, readers can extract valuable lessons that can be applied to their own situations.

Key insights include the importance of adaptability, innovative thinking, effective communication, and a strong community. As individuals and organizations face ongoing challenges and uncertainties, these principles can serve as a roadmap for navigating the unknown and turning adversity into opportunity.

Chapter 7: Embracing Continuous Learning

In an ever-evolving world, the ability to learn continuously is essential for navigating uncertainty and adapting to new challenges. This chapter focuses on fostering a mindset of lifelong learning, emphasizing the importance of seeking knowledge and embracing new experiences as vital strategies for personal and professional growth.

The Importance of Lifelong Learning

Lifelong learning refers to the ongoing, voluntary, and self-motivated pursuit of knowledge for personal or professional development. In today's fast-paced environment, where change is the only constant, the ability to learn continuously can significantly enhance one's adaptability and resilience.

1. **Adapting to Change**: The rapid pace of technological advancements, shifting job markets, and changing societal norms means that skills can quickly become outdated. Lifelong learning equips individuals with the tools necessary to adapt and thrive in an uncertain world.
2. **Fostering Innovation**: Continuous learning promotes creativity and innovation. By exposing oneself to new ideas, perspectives, and experiences, individuals can develop innovative solutions to complex problems.
3. **Enhancing Employability**: In a competitive job market,

having a commitment to lifelong learning demonstrates to employers that an individual is proactive, adaptable, and capable of growth, making them a valuable asset to any organization.

4. **Boosting Confidence**: Acquiring new skills and knowledge can enhance self-confidence and empower individuals to take on new challenges, ultimately leading to personal and professional fulfillment.

Cultivating a Lifelong Learning Mindset

Developing a mindset of continuous learning involves recognizing the value of knowledge and embracing opportunities for growth. Here are several strategies to cultivate this mindset:

1. **Adopt a Growth Mindset**: A growth mindset, as defined by psychologist Carol Dweck, is the belief that abilities and intelligence can be developed through dedication and hard work. Individuals with a growth mindset are more likely to embrace challenges, learn from criticism, and persist in the face of setbacks.
    - **Actionable Tip**: Challenge negative self-talk and replace it with positive affirmations that emphasize your capacity for growth. For example, instead of thinking, "I can't learn this," reframe it to "I can learn this with practice."
2. **Set Learning Goals**: Establish specific, measurable, achievable, relevant, and time-bound (SMART) learning goals to create a clear roadmap for your educational journey. This could include pursuing formal education, attending workshops, or dedicating time each week to self-study.
    - **Actionable Tip**: Identify one new skill you'd like to acquire in the next six months and outline the steps needed to achieve it. Break the process down into manageable tasks and set deadlines

to keep yourself accountable.

3. **Seek Diverse Learning Opportunities**: Embrace various learning formats, such as online courses, webinars, podcasts, books, and hands-on experiences. Diversifying your learning sources can provide a richer understanding of topics and expose you to different viewpoints.
    - **Actionable Tip**: Create a list of learning resources that interest you, including specific courses, books, and podcasts. Set a goal to explore at least one new resource each month.
4. **Cultivate Curiosity**: Nurturing a sense of curiosity about the world can enhance your learning journey. Approach new topics with an open mind and a desire to explore and understand.
    - **Actionable Tip**: Dedicate time each week to explore a subject outside your comfort zone. This could be through reading articles, watching documentaries, or attending lectures.
5. **Engage in Reflective Learning**: Reflect on your experiences and the knowledge you acquire. Reflective learning encourages deeper understanding and helps solidify new concepts.
    - **Actionable Tip**: Keep a learning journal where you record insights gained from your experiences and studies. Reflect on what you learned, how it applies to your life, and how you can continue to grow.

Embracing New Experiences

Embracing new experiences is a critical component of continuous learning. Actively seeking out new opportunities allows individuals to expand their horizons and gain practical knowledge. Here are some strategies for doing so:

1. **Participate in Workshops and Seminars**: Attending workshops and seminars can provide hands-on experience and networking opportunities with like-minded individuals.

    - **Actionable Tip**: Research local or online workshops relevant to your interests or career goals and commit to attending at least one in the next few months.
2. **Join Professional Organizations**: Becoming a member of professional organizations can offer access to resources, networking opportunities, and continued education.
    - **Actionable Tip**: Identify one or two organizations related to your field and consider joining. Attend their events or webinars to expand your network and knowledge base.
3. **Volunteer for New Roles or Projects**: Taking on new responsibilities at work or in community organizations can provide valuable learning experiences. Volunteering for projects outside your usual scope can also expose you to new skills and perspectives.
    - **Actionable Tip**: Look for volunteer opportunities in your workplace or community that align with your interests. Commit to at least one new role or project in the upcoming year.
4. **Travel and Cultural Experiences**: Traveling to new places and experiencing different cultures can offer invaluable learning opportunities. Engaging with diverse communities broadens your perspective and enhances your understanding of the world.
    - **Actionable Tip**: Plan a trip to a place you've never visited, whether it's a different city or country. Use the experience to learn about the local culture, customs, and ways of life.
5. **Pursue Hobbies and Interests**: Exploring hobbies and interests outside your professional life can lead to personal growth and development. Engaging in activities you're passionate about can spark creativity and offer new perspectives.
    - **Actionable Tip**: Identify a hobby you've always wanted to pursue and dedicate time each week to explore it, whether it's

painting, cooking, or learning a musical instrument.

Overcoming Barriers to Continuous Learning

While embracing continuous learning is essential, it's also important to recognize potential barriers that may hinder this journey. Here are some common challenges and strategies to overcome them:

1. **Time Constraints**: Many people feel they lack the time to dedicate to learning due to busy schedules.
    - **Strategy**: Prioritize learning by scheduling dedicated time blocks for educational activities. Even small increments of time, such as 15-30 minutes a day, can accumulate and lead to significant learning.
2. **Fear of Failure**: Fear of making mistakes or failing can deter individuals from taking on new challenges.
    - **Strategy**: Reframe failure as an opportunity for growth. Embrace the idea that making mistakes is a natural part of the learning process, and each setback can lead to valuable lessons.
3. **Complacency**: Sometimes, individuals may become complacent in their current knowledge or skills, believing there is no need for further learning.
    - **Strategy**: Regularly assess your skills and knowledge, identifying areas for improvement. Set new learning goals to keep yourself challenged and engaged.
4. **Lack of Motivation**: Staying motivated can be challenging, especially when faced with obstacles or setbacks.
    - **Strategy**: Connect your learning goals to your larger life vision and purpose. Remembering why you want to learn can reignite your motivation during challenging times.

Conclusion: The Journey of Lifelong Learning

Embracing continuous learning is a lifelong journey that enriches our lives and equips us with the skills necessary to navigate uncertainty. By adopting a growth mindset, setting learning goals, and seeking new experiences, individuals can foster an environment of continuous growth.

As readers reflect on their learning journeys, they are encouraged to embrace challenges, learn from experiences, and remain open to new opportunities. The process of learning is not just about acquiring knowledge; it's about personal transformation, resilience, and preparing to navigate the unknown. By committing to lifelong learning, individuals can become catalysts in their own lives, empowering themselves to adapt, thrive, and contribute to the world around them.

Chapter 8: Sustaining Momentum in Uncertain Times

In the face of uncertainty and adversity, maintaining momentum is crucial for personal and professional growth. This chapter focuses on strategies to sustain motivation, navigate challenges, and develop habits that promote long-term success, helping readers remain resilient in their journey through the unknown.

The Importance of Sustaining Momentum

Momentum refers to the drive and energy that propel individuals forward, enabling them to overcome obstacles and pursue their goals. In uncertain times, it can be easy to lose motivation or feel overwhelmed, making it essential to cultivate habits and practices that foster resilience and persistence.

1. **Enhancing Resilience**: Sustaining momentum helps individuals build resilience, allowing them to bounce back from setbacks and continue working towards their goals.
2. **Fostering Consistency**: Maintaining a consistent pace in pursuing goals can lead to incremental progress, even in the face of challenges.
3. **Strengthening Commitment**: Staying motivated reinforces a commitment to personal and professional development, helping individuals navigate uncertainty with confidence.

Strategies for Sustaining Momentum

1. Set Clear and Realistic Goals

Having well-defined, achievable goals provides a roadmap for progress. Clear goals help maintain focus and direction, making it easier to sustain momentum.

- **Actionable Tip**: Break larger goals into smaller, manageable tasks. Create a timeline for accomplishing each task to track progress and celebrate small wins along the way.

2. Establish Routines and Habits

Creating daily routines and habits can enhance productivity and support sustained momentum. Routines provide structure and consistency, helping individuals stay engaged and focused on their goals.

- **Actionable Tip**: Identify key habits that contribute to your success, such as setting aside time for focused work, practicing mindfulness, or engaging in regular exercise. Commit to integrating these habits into your daily routine.

3. Cultivate a Positive Mindset

Maintaining a positive mindset is vital for sustaining momentum, especially during challenging times. A positive attitude can help individuals navigate difficulties with resilience and optimism.

- **Actionable Tip**: Practice gratitude by reflecting on the positive aspects of your life and accomplishments. Keep a gratitude journal to document daily or weekly reflections, which can boost your overall outlook.

4. Leverage Accountability and Support Systems

Accountability plays a significant role in maintaining motivation and progress. Having a support system in place can provide encouragement, feedback, and a sense of shared purpose.

- **Actionable Tip**: Seek out accountability partners, mentors, or support groups to share your goals and progress. Regular check-ins with these individuals can help keep you on track and motivated.

5. Embrace Flexibility and Adaptability

In uncertain times, the ability to adapt to changing circumstances is crucial for sustaining momentum. Flexibility allows individuals to pivot when faced with challenges and reassess their goals and strategies.

- **Actionable Tip**: Regularly review your goals and progress, and be open to adjusting your plans as needed. Embrace change as an opportunity for growth rather than a setback.

6. Celebrate Achievements and Milestones

Recognizing and celebrating achievements, no matter how small, reinforces motivation and helps sustain momentum. Celebrating progress fosters a sense of accomplishment and encourages continued effort.

- **Actionable Tip**: Establish a system for celebrating milestones, whether through personal rewards, sharing successes with friends or family, or documenting achievements in a journal.

7. Create a Vision Board

A vision board can serve as a visual reminder of your goals and aspirations, helping to maintain motivation and focus. By regularly visualizing your goals, you reinforce your commitment to achieving them.

- **Actionable Tip**: Spend time creating a vision board that represents your goals, dreams, and sources of inspiration. Place it in a visible location to serve as a daily reminder of your journey.

Developing Habits that Support Long-Term Success

1. Prioritize Self-Care

Taking care of your physical, mental, and emotional well-being is essential for sustaining momentum. Practicing self-care helps prevent burnout and ensures that you have the energy and focus needed to pursue your goals.

- **Actionable Tip**: Incorporate self-care practices into your routine, such as regular exercise, healthy eating, adequate sleep, and mindfulness practices. Prioritize downtime to recharge and reflect.

2. Continuously Seek Learning Opportunities

Embracing a mindset of continuous learning supports long-term success and helps sustain momentum. By seeking new knowledge and skills, you remain adaptable and ready to tackle challenges.

- **Actionable Tip**: Set aside time each week for learning activities, whether through reading, online courses, or workshops. Choose topics that align with your goals and interests.

3. Foster a Growth Mindset

Cultivating a growth mindset enables individuals to view challenges as opportunities for growth rather than obstacles. A growth mindset fosters resilience and motivates individuals to push through difficulties.

- **Actionable Tip**: Reflect on your responses to setbacks. Instead of focusing on what went wrong, consider what you can learn from the experience and how you can improve moving forward.

4. Engage in Reflection and Self-Assessment

Regular reflection and self-assessment can help individuals stay connected to their goals and progress. Reflecting on experiences allows you to identify patterns, strengths, and areas for improvement.

- **Actionable Tip**: Schedule regular reflection sessions, whether weekly or monthly, to review your progress, celebrate achievements, and reassess your goals. Consider journaling your thoughts during these sessions.

Overcoming Challenges to Sustaining Momentum

1. **Dealing with Distractions**: In a world filled with distractions, staying focused can be challenging.
    - **Strategy**: Identify common distractions and create strategies to minimize them. This might include setting specific work hours, using productivity apps, or creating a dedicated workspace.
2. **Addressing Burnout**: Continuous effort without adequate rest can lead to burnout, hampering progress.
    - **Strategy**: Recognize the signs of burnout and prioritize breaks and self-care. Schedule regular downtime to recharge and reflect on your goals.
3. **Combatting Negative Thoughts**: Negative thoughts can sap motivation and hinder progress.
    - **Strategy**: Practice mindfulness and cognitive restructuring techniques to challenge and reframe negative thoughts. Focus on constructive self-talk that reinforces your goals.

Conclusion: Momentum as a Catalyst for Success

Sustaining momentum amid uncertainty is a vital skill that empowers individuals to navigate challenges and achieve long-term success. By implementing strategies such as setting clear goals, establishing routines, and fostering a positive mindset, readers can cultivate habits that support their journey.

As they reflect on their progress and celebrate achievements, they are encouraged to embrace the journey of growth and remain committed to their goals. By understanding the importance of sustaining momentum and actively working to maintain it, individuals can emerge as resilient catalysts in their own lives, ready to navigate the unknown with confidence and purpose.

Chapter 9 Conclusion: Your Catalyst Journey

As we conclude "The Catalyst Code: Navigating the Unknown," it's essential to reinforce the key messages that have emerged throughout the book. Our journey through uncertainty can be daunting, but it also presents opportunities for growth, transformation, and self-discovery. Embracing this unknown landscape is not just a necessity; it's an invitation to cultivate resilience, foster connections, and become the catalysts of change in our own lives and communities.

Embracing Uncertainty

1. The Nature of Uncertainty: Throughout the chapters, we have explored the multifaceted nature of uncertainty. It is inherent in every aspect of life, whether in personal endeavors, professional pursuits, or broader societal shifts. Understanding that uncertainty is a natural part of the human experience is the first step towards embracing it.

- **Key Takeaway**: Recognize uncertainty as a catalyst for innovation and growth rather than a barrier. By reframing your perspective on uncertainty, you can cultivate a mindset that is open to possibilities.

2. The Catalyst Mindset: We discussed the importance of developing a catalyst mindset—one that embraces change, fosters resilience, and seeks continuous growth. This mindset equips you to navigate the unknown with confidence and adaptability.

- **Key Takeaway**: Embrace challenges as opportunities for learning. When you encounter setbacks, approach them with curiosity and a willingness to evolve.

Actionable Steps for Continuous Growth

1. Cultivating Resilience: Resilience is the cornerstone of navigating uncertainty. The strategies outlined in Chapter 2 emphasize the significance of developing resilience through adaptability, self-awareness, and a positive outlook.

- **Actionable Step**: Regularly practice self-reflection to identify your strengths and areas for growth. Engage in activities that challenge you while fostering your resilience.

2. Leveraging Networks: Building a supportive network is essential for navigating challenges. The connections you cultivate can provide guidance, encouragement, and diverse perspectives.

- **Actionable Step**: Identify individuals in your network who inspire and support you. Reach out to them for mentorship, collaboration, or simply to share experiences. Invest in these relationships to foster mutual growth.

3. Utilizing Tools for Decision-Making: Decision-making is a crucial aspect of navigating uncertainty. Chapter 3 provided frameworks and tools for assessing risks and making informed choices.

- **Actionable Step**: When faced with decisions, use techniques such as scenario planning or pros-and-cons analysis. These tools can help clarify your options and guide you toward more confident decisions.

4. Creative Problem-Solving: In uncertain times, innovative problem-solving is key. Embrace creative approaches and think outside the box to develop solutions.

- **Actionable Step**: Set aside time for brainstorming sessions, either individually or with your network. Encourage open dialogue and exploration of unconventional ideas.

The Journey Ahead

1. Lifelong Learning: The importance of continuous learning cannot be overstated. By seeking new knowledge and experiences, you position yourself to adapt and thrive in an ever-changing world.

- **Actionable Step**: Make a commitment to lifelong learning by engaging in regular educational activities, whether through formal courses, workshops, or self-directed study. Share your learning journey with others to inspire collective growth.

2. Sustaining Momentum: Maintaining motivation and momentum is vital for long-term success. The practices discussed in Chapter 8 can help you stay engaged and focused on your goals.

- **Actionable Step**: Create a personal accountability system. Share your goals with trusted individuals who can offer support and encouragement. Regularly check in with them to celebrate progress and reassess your objectives.

Empowering Your Role as a Catalyst

As you move forward on your journey, remember that you have the power to influence not only your own path but also the lives of those around you. By embodying the principles outlined in this book, you can become a catalyst for change in your community and beyond.

1. **Take Initiative**: Don't wait for opportunities to come to you. Actively seek out ways to contribute, support others, and drive positive change.
2. **Share Your Journey**: Your experiences and insights can inspire

others. Share your journey through writing, speaking, or mentoring. By doing so, you not only reinforce your own growth but also empower those around you.

3. **Be a Lifelong Catalyst**: The journey of navigating the unknown is ongoing. Embrace the mindset of a catalyst as a lifelong commitment to growth, learning, and transformation.

Final Reflection

In conclusion, your journey as a catalyst is uniquely yours, marked by challenges, triumphs, and countless opportunities for growth. Embrace the unknown with open arms, knowing that within it lies the potential for remarkable transformation.

As you step into this journey, carry with you the lessons learned and the strategies outlined in this book. Empower yourself to navigate uncertainty with confidence, resilience, and creativity. The world needs your unique contributions, and by becoming a catalyst, you can inspire change not only in your own life but also in the lives of others.

May your journey be filled with discovery, growth, and the unwavering belief that you are capable of navigating the unknown. Embrace your role as a catalyst and let your journey unfold.

Other books by the Author

MBBS @ ZERO COST

https://www.amazon.com/dp/B07F7PDYKK

Is the dream of becoming a doctor being crushed under the weight of ₹1 Crore in private college fees? The thought alone is enough to cause sleepless nights, forcing countless brilliant students and their families to wonder if this noble dream is even possible. You've seen the headlines, you've heard the stories, and now you feel that financial dread firsthand.

This isn't just about money; it's about the years of hard work, the sacrifices made, and the passion to heal—all at risk of being washed away by a tide of crippling debt. You watch as others are forced to compromise, take on life-altering loans, or worse, abandon their medical aspirations altogether. The path to a private MBBS degree can feel like a trap, locking your family's future in a decade-long financial struggle before your career even begins. The agitation is real, and the fear of failure is paralyzing.

But what if there was another way? A proven path to earning your white coat without the soul-crushing financial burden?

Introducing "MBBS @ ZERO COST"—the definitive guide to turning your medical dream into a debt-free reality. This book is the lifeline you've been searching for. It's not about magic; it's a strategic, step-by-step blueprint that demystifies the process of securing a coveted seat in a government medical college. Forget the lakhs and crores. Inside, you'll discover the insider secrets, preparation strategies, and crucial mistakes to avoid that separate the successful few from the rest. Stop agonizing over finances and start building your future. This book is your first, most critical prescription for a successful and affordable medical career. Your dream is possible, and this is how you achieve it.

ALL INDIA INSTITUTE OF MEDICAL SCIENCES

https://www.amazon.com/dp/B078Z7NTY6

Congratulations, future doctor!

You are one step closer to conquering the AIIMS MBBS Entrance Examination.

You hold in your hands the definitive guide to mastering the General Knowledge section of one of India's most competitive medical entrance exams. "ALL INDIA INSTITUTE OF MEDICAL SCIENCES: GENERAL KNOWLEDGE" is meticulously crafted to provide you with the most relevant, well-researched, and up-to-date information necessary to excel.

Authored by Dr. Raam Harvard, this book goes beyond simple facts and figures. It provides a strategic roadmap to understanding the patterns and priorities of the AIIMS exam.

Inside, you will discover:

• Focused Content: Target the exact GK topics and current affairs that frequently appear in the AIIMS exam, saving you valuable preparation time.

• Strategic Insights: Learn how to "Think Like a WINNER" with proven strategies that will give you a competitive edge.

• Expert Guidance: Benefit from the author's intimate secrets and deep understanding of the examination process to avoid common pitfalls.

• A Clear Path to Success: Follow the unique analysis in the second chapter to unlock a study method that can yield returns far greater than the investment in this book.

Stop wasting time on irrelevant material. This guide is your single, most reliable resource to build the confidence and knowledge required to ace the General Knowledge section. Embrace the mindset of a top-ranker and take the first definitive step toward a successful medical career at AIIMS. What is Psychology?: Mastering the Mind: Unlock the Mysteries, Discover the Insights, Behaviors and Emotions of Your Self, Partners, Relationships, friends, Relations, Competitors, Enemies and Others What is Psychology?: Mastering the Mind: Unlock the Mysteries, Discover the Insights, Behaviors and Emotions of Your Self,

Partners, Relationships, friends, Relations, Competitors, Enemies and Other.

DIGITAL Economy Millennium OPPORTUNITY

https://www.amazon.com/dp/1973378248

Are you digitally updated? The revolution is not coming. It is here.

Silently, relentlessly, the digital economy is reshaping our world. But its true potential is not found in the headlines about AI and self-driving cars. It is found in the quiet, monumental shift that is lifting hundreds of millions out of poverty and building the economic superpowers of tomorrow.

DIGITAL Economy Millennium OPPORTUNITY is your guide to understanding this transformation from the front lines. Forget theory—this is the real-world story of how 1.3 billion people are leapfrogging into the future, turning the world's largest democracy into the world's largest digital lab.

With the expert analysis of Aiswarya Ram, MBA, this book dissects the mechanisms of this historic change, exploring:

- Constructive Digital Destruction: How legacy systems of corruption and exclusion were dismantled to make way for a transparent, digitally empowered society.
- Financial Inclusion at Scale: The strategy that ensured the "grass root downtrodden" were the primary beneficiaries of the new digital infrastructure.
- From Liability to Asset: The economic and philosophical shift that occurred when a nation's people became the engine of its digital growth through digitization and demonetization.

This is not just a reference book; it is a call to action. It provides an urgent roadmap for individuals, companies, and countries to adapt, thrive, and lead in the new global landscape. The future belongs to those who understand the forces detailed in these pages.

Digital is the future. Equip yourself for tomorrow, today.

$1000 Billion GOLD POT

HTTPS://WWW.AMAZON.com/dp/197670362X[1]

Unlock the Trillion-Dollar Opportunity Hidden in Plain Sight.

What if there was a hidden reservoir of national wealth, a trillion-dollar "Gold Pot" waiting to be claimed by those with the foresight to see it? In a world of economic uncertainty, renowned international finance expert Dr. Raam Harvard reveals the blueprint to one of the most significant wealth creation opportunities of the millennium.

This is the second book in the groundbreaking series that began with DIGITAL Economy Millennium OPPORTUNITY, delving deeper into the mechanisms of national prosperity and financial transformation.

In this concise and potent executive briefing, Dr. Harvard bypasses dense academic theory to deliver a direct, actionable framework for understanding and capitalizing on this emerging economic phenomenon. Drawing on his extensive experience as a leading Corporate Productivity Consultant and faculty for International Financial Reporting Standards (IFRS), he provides an unparalleled insider's view into the forces shaping the future of global finance.

Inside this strategic analysis, you will discover:

• The Anatomy of the "Gold Pot": A clear definition of this $1000 billion opportunity and the macroeconomic conditions that created it.

• The Three Pillars of Growth: Identify the key policy shifts, technological advancements, and industrial sectors poised for exponential growth.

• Strategic Investment Pathways: Understand where capital will flow and how to position yourself or your organization to benefit from this massive economic shift.

1. https://www.amazon.com/dp/197670362X

• Global Implications: Explore the ripple effects of this wealth creation event on international trade, investment, and monetary policy.

• A Roadmap for the Future: Gain the critical insights needed to navigate the new financial landscape, from the rise of digital currencies to the restructuring of traditional industries.

This is more than a book; it is a strategic advantage. It is for the investor seeking the next frontier, the policymaker shaping a nation's future, and the entrepreneur building the next global enterprise. The knowledge within these pages is the key to unlocking a new era of prosperity.

The opportunity of a millennium is here. Secure your strategic advantage today.

Demonetization - the QUANTUM JUMP

https://www.amazon.com/dp/B075RBVYVF

Imagine a single government decision rendering 86% of a nation's currency obsolete overnight. Was it a reckless gamble or a calculated leap into the future? Demonetization the QUANTUM JUMP argues it was the latter—a revolutionary catalyst that forever changed India's financial DNA.

This comprehensive analysis moves beyond the immediate shockwaves to reveal the long-term strategic thinking behind one of the most audacious economic experiments in modern history. Journey from the ancient Vedic system of currency to the future of a cashless "E-Life," and uncover the hidden architecture of this global phenomenon. The book dissects the legacy systems of black money, tax evasion, and real estate that the "Quantum Jump" was designed to disrupt, offering a clear-eyed look at the policy's consequences—the good, the bad, and the ugly.

Through insightful analysis and compelling stories, you will connect the dots of India's new economy and understand the profound structural shifts that are now underway. This is not just a book about a single policy; it is a guide to understanding revolutionary economic change, the future of money, and the bold vision shaping the world's largest democracy. Are you ready to grasp the full impact of the world's most disruptive financial shift?

DEMONETISATION: SUCCESS or FAILURE?

https://www.amazon.com/dp/B07CMSCZQ6

On the night of 8 November 2016, India witnessed a monetary shock of unprecedented scale. In a televised address, Prime Minister Narendra Modi announced that with just four hours' notice, the nation's two largest currency denominations—the 500 and 1,000 rupee notes—would be rendered worthless. This single act invalidated 86% of the cash in circulation, triggering a seismic event that brought the world's largest democracy to a virtual standstill.

Was this a masterstroke against corruption or a monumental mismanagement of the economy? DEMONETISATION: SUCCESS or FAILURE? provides the definitive, balanced analysis of one of modern India's most audacious and controversial policies.

The government's objectives were ambitious and, over time, evolved significantly. This book meticulously dissects each stated goal against the hard evidence, revealing a complex and often contradictory legacy:

• The War on Black Money: The primary stated goal was to unearth vast troves of illicit, untaxed cash and destroy counterfeit currency used to finance terrorism. Yet, the policy's effectiveness was immediately questioned when a staggering 99.3% of the demonetised currency was returned to the banking system, prompting many economists to declare this core objective a failure. This book examines why the initial assumptions about black money—that it is primarily held in cash—were flawed from the start.

• The Digital Revolution: As the initial narrative faltered, the focus shifted to transforming India into a "cashless" or "less-cash" society. This book quantifies the undeniable success of this secondary objective, detailing the explosive growth in digital payments, the widespread adoption of the Unified Payments Interface (UPI), and the significant push toward the formalization of the economy.

• Expanding the Tax Base: Proponents point to a tangible increase in tax compliance, with the number of income tax returns filed growing by 24.7% in the year following demonetisation. The analysis within explores whether this expansion was a direct and sustainable result of the policy or a temporary outcome of forcing cash into formal channels.

While some hailed these outcomes as long-term victories, they came at a tremendous cost. The book provides a sober assessment of the policy's severe and far-reaching consequences:

• The Economic Shockwave: The sudden liquidity crunch triggered a sharp contraction in economic activity. This analysis delves into the quantitative data, exploring estimates from the Economic Survey and prominent economists who projected a decline in GDP growth ranging from 0.25% to as high as 2%. The book investigates the slowdown in key sectors like manufacturing, real estate, and construction, providing a clear picture of the macroeconomic damage.

• The Human Cost: Beyond the macroeconomic data lies a story of immense human hardship. The policy disproportionately impacted the cash-reliant informal sector, which employs over 85% of India's workforce. This book gives voice to the daily wage laborers, small farmers, and micro-entrepreneurs who faced devastating losses of income and employment, with some estimates suggesting 1.5 million jobs were lost in the immediate aftermath.

• The Great Intellectual Divide: The policy ignited a fierce debate among the world's leading economic minds. This book navigates the dissenting views of Nobel laureate Amartya Sen, who called it a "despotic act," and former central bank governor Raghuram Rajan, who warned of the costs, contrasting them with the supportive arguments of economists like Jagdish Bhagwati, who hailed it as a "courageous reform".

DEMONETISATION: SUCCESS or FAILURE? moves beyond partisan rhetoric to deliver a data-driven, nuanced verdict. It unpacks the complex interplay of economics and politics, answering the crucial question that continues to haunt policymakers and citizens alike: How do we measure the true legacy of a policy that was, for many, an economic disaster but was simultaneously perceived as a political masterstroke? This book is an essential resource for anyone seeking to understand this pivotal moment in India's history.

BITCOIN SECRETS : ALL YOU MUST KNOW

https://www.amazon.com/dp/B078BJ7RCX

Unlock the Power of Bitcoin: Your Guide to Navigating the Future of Money is Here.

Feeling left behind by the Bitcoin revolution? Are you overwhelmed by technical terms, conflicting advice, and the fear of making a costly mistake? You're not alone. The world of cryptocurrency can seem like an exclusive club, but "BITCOIN SECRETS" is your personal invitation to join with confidence.

This is not just another book about what Bitcoin is. This is a practical, step-by-step guide on what to do. Forget the get-rich-quick hype. This book provides the foundational knowledge and actionable strategies you need to treat Bitcoin as a serious technological and financial tool.

Inside "BITCOIN SECRETS," you will discover:

• The Core Secrets of the Blockchain: Understand in simple, plain English how the technology actually works and why it's poised to change everything.

• The Smart Way to Buy & Sell: A step-by-step walkthrough of acquiring your first Bitcoin, avoiding high fees, and choosing the right exchanges.

• Fort Knox Security Protocols: Learn the crucial secrets to securing your digital assets. We cover cold storage, hardware wallets, and the common pitfalls that leave others vulnerable.

• Decoding the Market: Uncover the patterns behind market cycles, understand the impact of "halving," and learn to separate genuine trends from market noise.

• Beyond Bitcoin: A clear overview of how Bitcoin's success has paved the way for thousands of other cryptocurrencies and the wider world of DeFi (Decentralized Finance).

• Common Mistakes and How to Avoid Them: Learn from the errors of others to protect your time, money, and peace of mind.

Whether you're a complete beginner who has never bought a single satoshi, or you've dabbled in crypto and want to deepen your understanding, "BITCOIN SECRETS" is the clear, concise, and indispensable resource you've been searching for.

Don't just watch the future of finance unfold—be a part of it. Scroll up and unlock the secrets today!

BUY BITCOIN with CREDIT CARD

https://www.amazon.com/dp/B077Z3WHFC

Ready to finally own your first Bitcoin but overwhelmed by the complexity? You're not alone.

The world of cryptocurrency can feel like an exclusive club, filled with technical jargon and confusing platforms. Many potential investors feel left behind, worried about making a costly mistake. But what if there was a simple, familiar way to get started in minutes?

In "BUY BITCOIN with CREDIT CARD," you'll discover the most straightforward path to entering the digital asset market. This book demystifies the entire process, cutting through the noise to provide a clear, secure, and easy-to-follow roadmap. It's designed specifically for the absolute beginner who wants to act now, using a tool they already have in their wallet.

Inside this essential guide, you will learn:

• Step-by-Step Walkthroughs: Clear, illustrated instructions on how to purchase Bitcoin from reputable platforms using your credit card.

- Choosing the Right Exchange: A breakdown of the best and safest platforms that accept credit card payments, comparing their pros and cons.
- Navigating Fees and Limits: Understand exactly what you'll pay and how to minimize costs, so there are no surprises.
- Security First: Crucial tips on how to secure your new digital assets immediately after purchase to protect them from hackers and theft.
- Common Pitfalls to Avoid: Learn from the mistakes of others so you can invest with confidence and avoid rookie errors.
- What to Do Next: A brief introduction to crypto wallets and what your options are after you've made your first purchase.

This book is not for crypto experts. It's for the everyday person—the student, the professional, the retiree—who is curious about Bitcoin and wants a safe, simple, and immediate way to get started.

Don't let confusion be the barrier to your financial future. Scroll up to begin your crypto journey today!

Don't miss out!

Visit the website below and you can sign up to receive emails whenever Dr.Raam Harvard publishes a new book. There's no charge and no obligation.

https://books2read.com/r/B-A-OLZW-HYDYG

BOOKS 2 READ

Connecting independent readers to independent writers.

Did you love *The Catalyst Code*? Then you should read *The Potential Trap*[2] by Dr.Raam Harvard!

[3]

Are you tired of chasing your "full potential," only to feel more burnt out, anxious, and overworked than ever?

You've followed the advice, embraced the hustle culture, and strived for perfection. Yet, instead of fulfillment, you're left with a nagging sense of failure and the constant pressure to do more. If the endless race to improve has left you feeling like you're never enough, you're not alone. You're caught in The Potential Trap.

This book exposes the counterintuitive truth: our society's obsession with reaching an idealized "full potential" is a toxic myth. It's the hidden source of our anxiety, fueling the perfectionism and burnout that leave us feeling stuck and overwhelmed.

---

2. https://books2read.com/u/3knD8R

3. https://books2read.com/u/3knD8R

The Potential Trap is the refreshing, honest anti-self-help guide for anyone who is skeptical of the usual "positive thinking" advice. It provides a practical roadmap to break free from the cycle of self-criticism and exhaustion.

Inside, you will discover how to:

Overcome perfectionism by letting go of unrealistic expectations and embracing the power of "good enough."Achieve lasting **burnout recovery** with sustainable strategies for both your work and personal life.Cultivate genuine **self-acceptance** and stop seeking external validation.Build a life of purpose and contentment by **redefining success** on your own terms.

For readers of *The Subtle Art of Not Giving a F*ck* and *The Gifts of Imperfection*, this book is an actionable alternative to the toxic productivity mindset. If you're ready to escape the pressure, reclaim your energy, and finally find peace with who you are, it's time to learn what lies beyond The Potential Trap.

Read more at https://drraam.com/.

Also by Dr.Raam Harvard

Money

Demonetization the QUANTUM JUMP

DIGITAL Economy Millennium OPPORTUNITY

Psychology

What is Psychology?: Unlocking Practical Tools for Growth

The 7-Figure Network

The Catalyst Code

The Potential Trap

Watch for more at https://drraam.com/.

About the Author

Dr. Raam Harvard is a well-known author.

His published books include MBBS @ ZERO COST, All India Institute Of Medical Sciences, DIGITAL Economy Millennium OPPORTUNITY, $1000 Billion GOLD POT, Demonetization the QUANTUM JUMP, Demonetisation: SUCCESS or FAILURE?, BITCOIN SECRETS , BUY BITCOIN with CREDIT CARD, etc.

He was bestowed with the International Business Excellence Award and the Best Entrepreneur Award.

Dr. Raam Harvard is faculty for International Financial Reporting Standards (IFRS), International Accounting & Auditing Standards (IAAS), Fraud &Forensic Audit, COBIT standard, ISO standard, Corporate Finance Taxation, Foreign Trade, Information Technology Audit, Java Programming, Oracle, Valuation of assets, Audit of Public Sector Undertakings, and Public-Private Partnerships.

He is a leading Corporate Productivity Consultant (TopmostConsultants.com) specialized in Corporate Training for Productivity improvement/Scaling-up and development of wealth of individuals and organizations.

He is also Professional Member of International Solar Energy Society, International Expert Network (IEN), Patron- Builders Association of India, Fellow- Solar Energy Society of India, and Life Fellow- Professional Counseling Psychologists Association.

He serves as Chairman of M/s V V I P Wealth Advisors Worldwide, a Triple ISO accredited Organization and the Poverty Eradication Charitable Trust(Triple ISO).

He is an honorable member of Gemological Institute of America (GIA), Federation of Exporters Organization (FIEO), Gem & Jewelry Export Promotion Council, Gem &Jewelry Federation, Confederation of Indian Industry, Environment Council and several other reputed organizations.

He is Guest Faculty for International students.

Ms. Aiswarya Ram, a Model , and winner of Best Women Entrepreneur Award, with MBA in Information Systems, published research papers in **International Journal of Commerce and Innovations**, co- authors several books, including Demonetization_the QUANTUM JUMP, DIGITAL Economy Millennium OPPORTUNITY, etc.

She services as honorary secretary to the triple ISO accredited Poverty Eradication Charitable Trust. Her efforts in women emancipation programs contributed the main thread.

RunToTOP.com

Read more at https://drraam.com/.

About the Publisher

"Knowledge is the most powerful tool for change." — Dr. Raam Harvard

Poverty Eradication Trust (Triple ISO)

Impact Publishing with a Purpose. Certified. Trusted. Triple ISO Standard.

Welcome to the powerhouse behind this book — **Poverty Eradication Trust (PET)** — where words don't just entertain, they **ignite minds, uplift lives, and spark real change.**

We're not your regular publishing house.We are **a purpose-driven, globally certified Triple ISO organization**, built on a mission:**Educate.Empower.Eradicate Poverty.**

Where Stories Change Lives We believe in the power of stories to transform hearts, minds—and the world! We're not just about creating unforgettable books; we're on a mission to eradicate poverty, one page at a time.

A Legacy of Impact Founded with a vision to blend literary excellence with social good, we pour our heart into every story we publish. From pulse-pounding thrillers to soul-stirring romances, our books are crafted to captivate, inspire, and leave you craving more. But that's not all—every purchase you make supports our initiatives to uplift communities, fund education, and break the cycle of poverty worldwide.

Why Readers Love Us Readers adore our curated collection of viral, unputdownable stories that keep them up all night. You can trust that every book meets the highest standards of quality, sustainability, and ethical impact. Join a global community of book lovers who are making a difference.

What We Publish

From **gripping fiction thrillers** that race your pulse, to **mind-shifting non-fiction** and **life-transforming educational content**, we craft and curate content that hits hard, sticks deep, and **sells worldwide**.

We're behind:

50+ Fiction Thrillers20+ Non-Fiction Game-Changers80+ Online Psychology CoursesSeries on AI, Cybersecurity, Bitcoin, and more!

All designed to **educate, entertain, and empower.**

Who We Serve

We don't just cater to readers — we serve:**Entrepreneurs & Students** looking to learn smarter.**Thriller Fans** who crave adrenaline and intrigue.**Corporates** seeking psychological edge through our consulting and content.

Where to Find Us

Fiction & Thrillers: Online Courses: Consulting Services: Author Branding & Books:

Join the Movement

We're more than a publisher — we're a **revolution** in storytelling and psychology-led transformation.

Follow us to discover our latest releases, behind-the-scenes magic, and the incredible impact your support creates. Share your reading journey with #PETBooks and let's spark a revolution—because great stories can change the world, and together, we're creating a brighter future!

Be part of our tribe:

Poverty Eradication Trust

Triple ISO Certified | Impact Driven | Story Powered"*Because books should do more than sit on shelves — they should build futures.*"

Thank You for Reading with Purpose!

9 789349 611610

Printed at Repro India Ltd.